W9-BAP-055

Project Otter

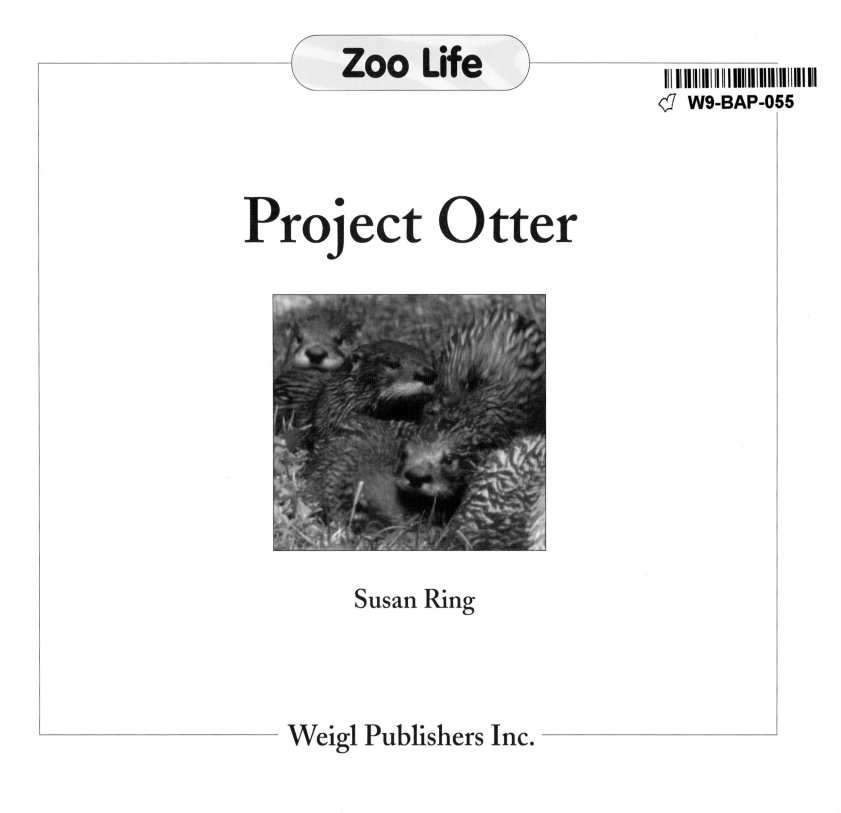

Susan Ring

Weigl Publishers Inc.

Editor
Diana Marshall

Design and Layout
Warren Clark
Bryan Pezzi

Copy Editor
Heather Kissock

Photo Researcher
Tina Schwartzenberger

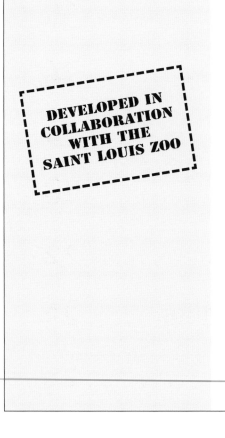

DEVELOPED IN COLLABORATION WITH THE SAINT LOUIS ZOO

Published by Weigl Publishers Inc.
123 South Broad Street, Box 227
Mankato, MN 56002 USA
Web site: www.weigl.com

Library of Congress Cataloging-in-Publication Data available upon request from the
publisher. Fax (507) 388-2746 for the attention of the Publishing Records Department.

ISBN 1-59036-059-1

Printed in the United States of America
1 2 3 4 5 6 7 8 9 0   06 05 04 03 02

Photograph Credits
Every reasonable effort has been made to trace ownership and to obtain permission
to reprint copyright material. The publishers would be pleased to have any errors
or omissions brought to their attention so that they may be corrected in
subsequent printings.

Cover: baby river otter (D. Robert Franz); **Steve Bircher/Saint Louis Zoo:** pages 3,
5 left, 6, 7 left, 11 left, 12, 14, 17 far right, 21 right, 22 top; **Ken W. Davis/Tom Stack &
Associates:** page 19; **Chuck Dresner/Saint Louis Zoo:** title page, pages 4, 8, 9 left, 10,
11 right, 15; **D. Robert & Lorri Franz/CORBIS/MAGMA:** pages 5 right, 18; **Don Grall/MaXx
Images:** page 16; **Thomas Kitchin/Tom Stack & Associates:** pages 7 right, 13, 21 left, 22
bottom; **Joe McDonald/Tom Stack & Associates:** pages 17 far left, 17 left, 17 middle, 23;
Gary Milburn/Tom Stack & Associates: page 20; **Brian Parker/Tom Stack & Associates:**
page 9 right; **Peter Worth/Papilio/CORBIS/MAGMA:** page 17 right.

Contents

Babies are Born

Hidden in a cozy **den** at the Saint Louis Zoo, a litter of otter pups was born in March. **Zookeepers** do not know the exact day the babies were born. At first, they did not even know how many pups were born. The mother otter kept her pups in her underground den for about 8 weeks. During that time, she took care of her babies in private.

Zoo Issues

Should newborn baby animals be put on public display?

At the Saint Louis Zoo, otters are born in a natural setting. They do not meet a zookeeper until they are about 8 weeks old.

Like all otters, the four pups looked like tiny adult otters when they were born. They had thick, brown fur and small whiskers. Like all newborn otters, they were born with their eyes closed. The pups did not open their eyes until they were about 5 weeks old. They were also born without teeth. Still, the four baby otters knew how to nurse. They were able to drink their mother's milk right away.

- Baby otters are called pups.

- Several baby otters born at one time to one mother is called a litter.

- A mother river otter usually gives birth to between two and five pups in one litter.

- At birth, pups are about 9 inches long. Their tail is about 2.5 inches long. They weigh about 4 ounces.

- Mother otters lick their pups clean after they are born.

- Baby otters nurse for 3 to 4 months.

- There are sea otters and river otters. The new pups at the Saint Louis Zoo are North American river otters.

About 2 months after the otters were born, zookeepers were excited to see four pups crawl out of the den into the otter yard.

Meet the Babies

The pups were not named by Saint Louis Zoo's zookeepers because they were moved to other zoos before they were 1 year old. Unless animals live at the zoo for a long time, they are given only a six-digit number. These numbers help keep track of the zoo's animals.

Zookeepers knew little about the pups until they were 6 months old. At that time, the zoo **veterinarian** gave them their first checkup. The pups were weighed and **vaccinated**.

Zookeepers did not know that three pups were male and one was female until they were 6 months old.

Zoo Issues

Should baby zoo animals share enclosures with their mother? Why?

The baby otters were helpless until they were about 6 weeks old. They made chirping sounds to communicate with their mother. These sounds let their mother know they were hungry or scared. At 6 weeks of age, the pups began to walk. They were slow and shaky at first. The pups were not yet ready to leave the den and try the water in the otter **enclosure**.

■ The pups continued to drink their mother's milk until they were ready to learn to catch fish.

Otter in the Water

Otters are super swimmers. They learn this skill from their mother. The pups learned to swim in shallow water. Their mother watched to make sure they were safe. Their first swimming lessons were short because the pups could not control their arms and legs. Little by little, the four baby otters became more comfortable in the pool. Soon, they were swimming, splashing, diving, and gliding through the deep water. The pups' play activities taught them hunting skills. The pups formed **bonds** with their mother and each other.

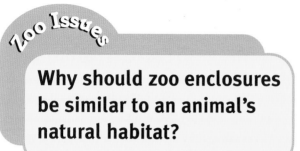

Zoo Issues

Why should zoo enclosures be similar to an animal's natural habitat?

At first, the pups were afraid to swim. Their mother encouraged them into the pool, often carrying them across in her mouth.

The baby otters loved winter. They would chase each other and slide down snowy hills on their stomachs.

Otters are very playful, curious animals. The new pups enjoyed sliding down muddy banks into the water. They played with toys and sticks in the otter yard. They loved to wrestle, and play tag and hide-and-seek. They were full of energy. They juggled pebbles and shells in their paws. After playing, the pups liked to stretch out on riverbanks in the sun.

- Otters can dive 60 feet deep. They can stay underwater for about 4 minutes.

- Otters are the fastest swimmers of all the **mammals** that live in fresh water. They also float easily. They are powerful and graceful swimmers.

- Otters use their eyesight to catch fish in clear rivers and streams. In muddy water, they use their whiskers to find fish.

- River otters are found in a variety of water **habitats** including rivers, streams, ponds, lakes, and marshes.

Meet the Parents

The new litter's mother was born on March 22, 1995 at the Saint Louis Zoo. Zookeepers named her Scamper because she was active and playful. She was always swimming and running around. The pups' father was born on April 4, 1989, at the Minnesota Zoo. He was moved to the Saint Louis Zoo in 1997. He was named Hercules by the zookeepers. They noticed that he liked to push the large, 50-pound den box all around his yard.

■ Scamper shares the yard with her mother, Louise, and Hercules.

Zoo Issues

Think of some reasons why zoo animals may need to be separated.

Scamper and Hercules were carefully introduced to each other. Hercules was put inside a kennel, called a "howdy cage." The howdy cage was placed in Scamper's yard. This let them get used to each other safely and slowly. Zookeepers noticed that the otters liked each other. Scamper and Hercules mated in the spring. They stayed together in the yard until December. Hercules was moved to a separate enclosure, away from pregnant Scamper. He was not reunited with her until 9 months after she gave birth, when the pups were no longer with her. This was Scamper's first litter.

The baby otters were raised only by their mother, Scamper.

Preparing for Pups

Zookeepers knew that Scamper was pregnant. They noticed a change in her actions. She was **aggressive** toward the other otters and the zookeepers. Scamper spent much of her time eating and staying inside her den. Zookeepers realized she was preparing her den for the pups. They knew that in a few weeks, a litter of baby otters would be born.

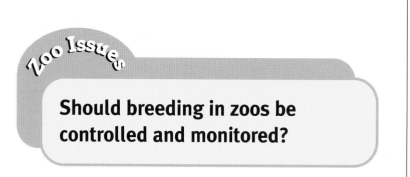

Zoo Issues

Should breeding in zoos be controlled and monitored?

When Scamper was pregnant, she was hostile toward Hercules and Louise.

- Male and female river otters are ready to mate when they are 2 years old.

- In the wild, river otter pups stay with their mother until a new litter is born in the spring. At about 1 year of age, the young will leave the group.

- Otters can grow to be 3 to 4.5 feet long, including their tail. An otter's tail can be 1 to 1.5 feet long.

- River otters use their long, flat tails for balance on land and for speed in the water.

Scamper, Hercules, and the pups are monitored through a program called ARKS. ARKS stands for Animal Record Keeping System. About 500 zoos and wildlife centers worldwide use the ARKS program. Zoos use a computer system to keep track of their animals and to keep records of their **breeding programs**. They also share information about new zoo babies. ARKS helps protect animals, such as the North American river otter, from **extinction**.

The Zoo Crew

Zookeepers at the Saint Louis Zoo feed the otters daily. They clean the 40 foot wide by 40 foot long otter enclosure. Zookeepers also know each otter well enough to notice when one of them is sick. The zoo's veterinarians give the otters regular checkups. The veterinarians also give the otters medical treatments when they are sick. The **curator** makes sure that the enclosure is similar to the otters' natural habitat. Having the right plants, foods, and toys will keep the otters happy and healthy.

The Saint Louis Zoo's otter yard includes grassy banks, trees, shrubs, and a large pool and stream.

In the wild, mother otters teach their pups to dive for fish, frogs, water insects, and their favorite food—crayfish. At the Saint Louis Zoo, the otters are fed twice a day. In the morning, zookeepers feed them a special meat diet. In the afternoon, they feed the otters fish. By 10 weeks of age, the pups learned to follow their mother to where zookeepers feed the adult otters.

The baby otters learned not to fear the zookeepers. They knew that zookeepers bring food.

HOW CAN I BECOME A VOLUNTEER?

Zoo volunteers are knowledgeable, trained helpers. They teach visitors about animal behavior and **conservation** issues. Some zoos have student volunteer programs that run through the summer. Volunteers must have a passion for animals. They must also take a training course offered by the zoos. To volunteer, contact your local zoo.

ZOO RULES

Zoo visitors watch the otters play in their yard and swim in the pool. At the children's zoo, visitors can slide down a see-through chute in the center of the otters' pool. The otters swim, dive, and play around the chute. While the otters have learned that visitors are not a danger, visitors must follow the rules. Zoos have rules that help keep animals and visitors safe and healthy.

The Saint Louis Zoo's Rules:
1. Pets are not allowed in the zoo.
2. Do not feed the animals.
3. Bikes, skateboards, and scooters are not allowed on zoo grounds.
4. Do not play loud radios.
5. Laser lights are not allowed in the zoo.

Animal Gear

River otters are comfortable on land and in water. Their bodies are **streamlined** and powerful. Their sharp teeth grind shells and bones, and grip and tear fish. From their teeth to their feet, otters are built to be great fishers and strong, fast, swimmers.

Why is it important for zoo food to be similar to animals' food in the wild?

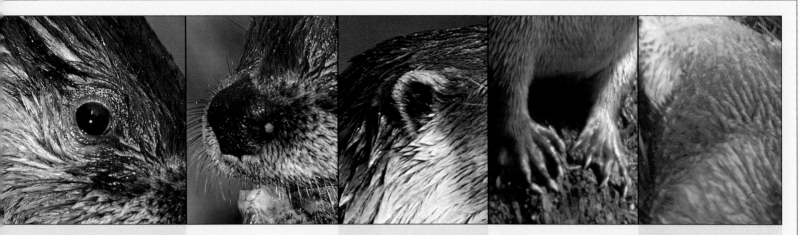

Eyes

Otters do not have very good eyesight. Instead, they rely on their ears on land and their whiskers in the water. Otters' eyes are placed near the top of their head. This helps the otters see above the surface of the water while they swim below.

Nose

River otters have large, black noses. River otters do not have fur on their noses. Their nostrils close up when under the water, to prevent water from entering. Their whiskers are very sensitive. They are used to detect movement in dark or muddy water.

Ears

Otters have tiny ears, but keen hearing. On land, river otters depend more on their hearing than their eyesight. Their ears have small flaps that close up when otters are underwater. This prevents water from entering their ears when otters swim and dive for food.

Paws

River otters have strong, webbed paws that help them move easily through the water. Sharp claws on all four paws help otters grip when they walk on land. Bumps on the bottom of their hind feet help otters grip slippery mud, snow, and ice.

Fur

Otters have thick, brown, oily fur. Natural oils in the fur trap warm air between the hairs. While their fur protects otters from cold water, it is not totally waterproof. If otters stay in the water too long, their fur can become wet and heavy.

In the Wild

River otters live near ponds, lakes, streams, and rivers. They make their homes along muddy banks. They construct a tunnel linking their den to the water. Otters enter their dens underwater. In the wild, river otters are most active at night. They play and feed until early morning. During the daytime, they rest in their underground dens. Otters are very social, and sometimes they will play right through the day.

Otters enjoy cold weather. Two layers of thick fur protect them from the cold.

River otters have large **home ranges**. Between 5 and 50 miles of **waterways** can serve as a home range. An otter will constantly move within that range, searching for food. Otters will avoid each other rather than fight over **territory**.

River otters dive to muddy river bottoms and pick out crayfish, clams, shrimps, insects, and frogs. On land, they eat small animals such as birds and rabbits, as well as plants.

River otters catch fish in their mouths while they swim.

Finding Fur

River otters have few enemies in the water. On land, they fear **predators** such as eagles and bears. Humans are their main enemy. Humans hunt and trap them for their thick fur. In 1800, about 65,000 river otters were trapped in North America. By 1904, river otters had completely disappeared from many states. Today, the river otter is not nationally **endangered**, but it is carefully protected.

Zoo Issues

How can zoos help wild animal populations?

Pollution and habitat loss have lowered river otter populations in the United States.

In 1980, there were less than 100 river otters in Missouri. During the next 10 years, the Saint Louis Zoo took part in a program that introduced many otters into the state from Louisiana. Now, the otter population is about 20,000. Five litters of river otters have already been born at the zoo. Another litter is on the way. The Saint Louis Zoo uses its breeding programs to help river otter populations in North America. Otters are even **reintroduced** into the wild.

The zoo educates the public on ways to preserve the river otters' habitat.

Otter Issues

Benefits of Zoo Life

- No danger from predators, hunting, competition, or habitat loss
- Regular food, play time, and medical care
- Can help educate the public about otters
- Can live a longer life
- Can be reintroduced into wild otter populations
- Is easier to research otters in zoos

Benefits of Life in the Wild

- More natural space in which to hunt and live
- Maintain diverse otter populations
- Daily mental and physical challenges, such as hunting
- Part of the natural web of life consisting of plants, predators, and prey
- Live complex lives
- Maintain independence

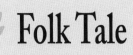

Folk Tale

Why the Otter is so Happy

A Native-American legend tells of Earth before humans. Only animals lived on the planet. The Sun was so far from Earth that there was no summer. The Animal Creator saw this, so he snared the Sun and brought it close to Earth. Unfortunately, the Sun was now too close. None of the animals were brave enough to free the Sun, except little Otter, whom the others did not like. Otter chewed through the leather of the snare, freeing the Sun. Otter was badly burned. To thank him, the Animal Creator gave Otter new strong teeth, tireless muscles, keen hearing, fine fur, and a powerful tail.

More Information

The Internet can lead you to some exciting information on otters. Try searching on your own, or visit the following Web sites:

American Zoo and Aquarium Association (AZA)
www.aza.org

Otters Page National Geographic
www.nationalgeographic.com/ottercam

PBS "Nature" Yellowstone Otters
www.pbs.org/wnet/nature/otters/river.html

Saint Louis Zoo www.stlzoo.org

CONSERVATION GROUPS
There are many organizations involved in otter research and conservation. You can get information on otters by writing to the following addresses:

INTERNATIONAL
International Otter
Survival Fund
Skye Environmental Centre Ltd.
Broadford, Isle of Skye
IV49 9AQ
Scotland

UNITED STATES
River Otter Alliance
6733 S. Locust Court
Englewood, Colorado
80112

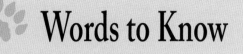

Words to Know

aggressive: forceful and protective

bonds: close relationships

breeding programs: producing babies by mating selected animals

conservation: the care and monitoring of animals and animal populations for their continued existence

curator: person in charge of an exhibit or a section of a zoo

den: like the shelter of a wild animal

enclosure: closed-in area that is designed to copy an animal's home in the wild

endangered: animals whose numbers are so low that they are at risk of disappearing from the wild

extinction: complete disappearance

gland: an organ in the body that produces scents

habitat: place in the wild where an animal naturally lives

home ranges: areas where an animal normally lives

mammals: warm-blooded animals

predators: animals that hunt and kill other animals for food

prey: animals that are hunted and killed for food

reintroduced: placed an animal or population back into a habitat

streamlined: smooth and sleek, able to move quickly through water or air

territory: area that an animal will defend as its own

vaccinated: given medicines to prevent diseases

veterinarian: animal doctor

waterways: bodies of water

zookeepers: people at a zoo who feed and take care of the animals

Index